Slava

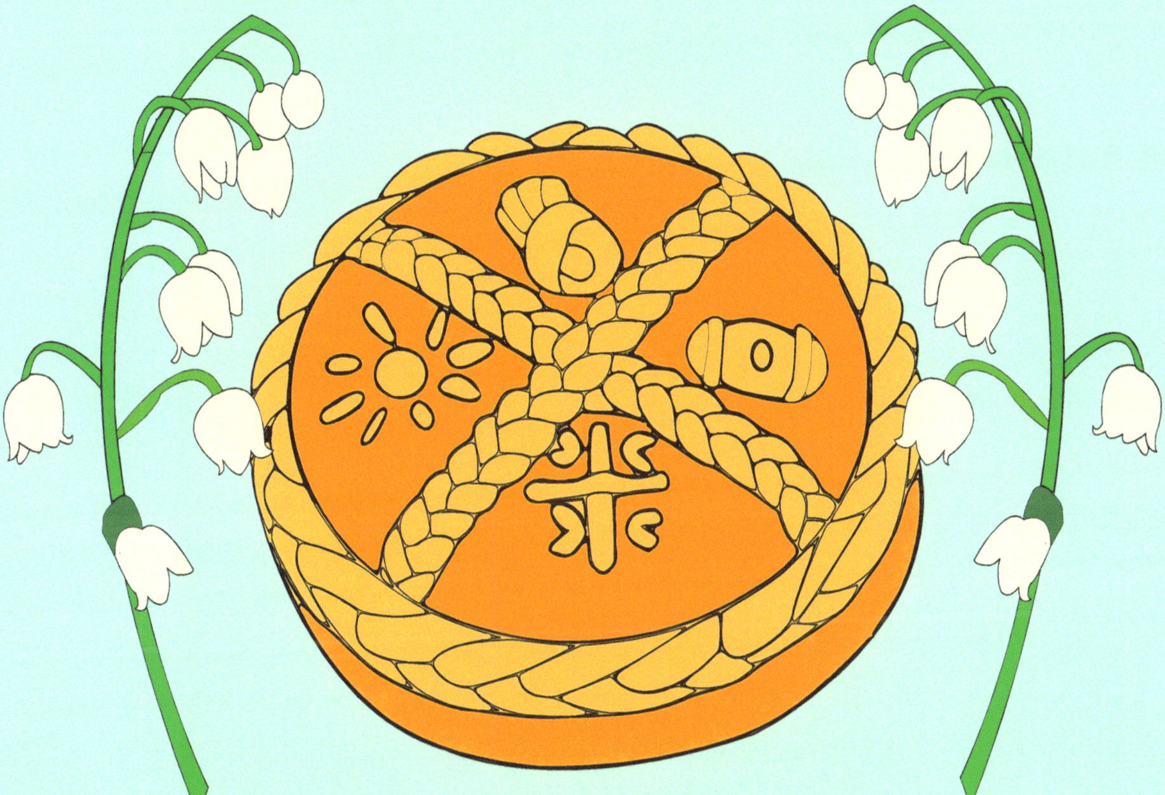

Written and illustrated by
Anisha Clay

About The Author

My name is Anisha Clay, and I hail from the beautiful land of Southern California. While I proudly embrace my Indian heritage, my husband's family roots trace back to Serbia.

Several years ago, our family embarked on a new chapter when we relocated from the tropical Hawaii to the vibrant community of Southern California. It was during this transition that I felt a strong desire to ensure that our children, the pillars of our future, would grow up embracing and understanding their Serbian customs, traditions, and religions.

In our quest to nurture our children's cultural identity, we were fortunate to cross paths with Father Predrag Bojovic, a Serbian Orthodox priest. From the moment we met him, Father Predrag graciously opened his heart and welcomed our family into the Serbian community with open arms.

With Father Predrag's invaluable oversight and support, I brought to life a book that celebrates Slava, immersing young readers in its vibrant colors, enchanting stories, and time-honored customs. It is my hope that this book will serve as a joyful tool for both children and adults to learn and appreciate the rich tapestry of Serbian culture.

Thank you for joining me on this remarkable journey. Together, let's celebrate diversity, nurture cultural understanding, and embrace the beauty of our shared human experiences. Enjoy the book, and may it inspire a love for traditions that transcend borders.

Warm regards, Anisha Clay

Every year Serbian families
across the world gather on a
special day to celebrate Slava,
a Serbian Orthodox tradition
used to give glory and thanks to the
family's patron saint.

Slava, like a golden thread,
links our past to our present,
our ancestors to our descendants.
An icon or picture of the
family saint is traditionally kept on the
East wall of the family room.

Slava marks one of the holiest and cheerful holidays celebrated by Serbs. Usually starting around early autumn, after Christmas and Easter. In Serbia, it is certainly a busy time for most families and supermarkets!

Families will be
carrying piles of food
in preparation for a
Delicious feast.

Unlike most holidays and customs, each family separately celebrates their dedicated
divine protector and saint, known as their Slava. This patron saint is passed down from the
head of the household to the children.

During **Slava**, families pray and perform religious rituals to remember their ancestors who celebrated the same saint for generations.
This saint blesses and protects the household and all their loved ones.

On the day of our saint's celebration, we put on our best outfits and attend the most important part of the Slava rituals, the church service.

Blessings of bread and wine are
given by the Father as the
family partakes in
HOLY COMMUNION

FLOUR
SUGAR

After the church service, we prepare for the Slava feast! It is important to have the icon of the patron saint, a Slava candle, Slava cake and yummy boiled wheat. The Slava cake is the focal point of the celebration. It is carefully baked and decorated with the Cross and the "Dove of Peace".

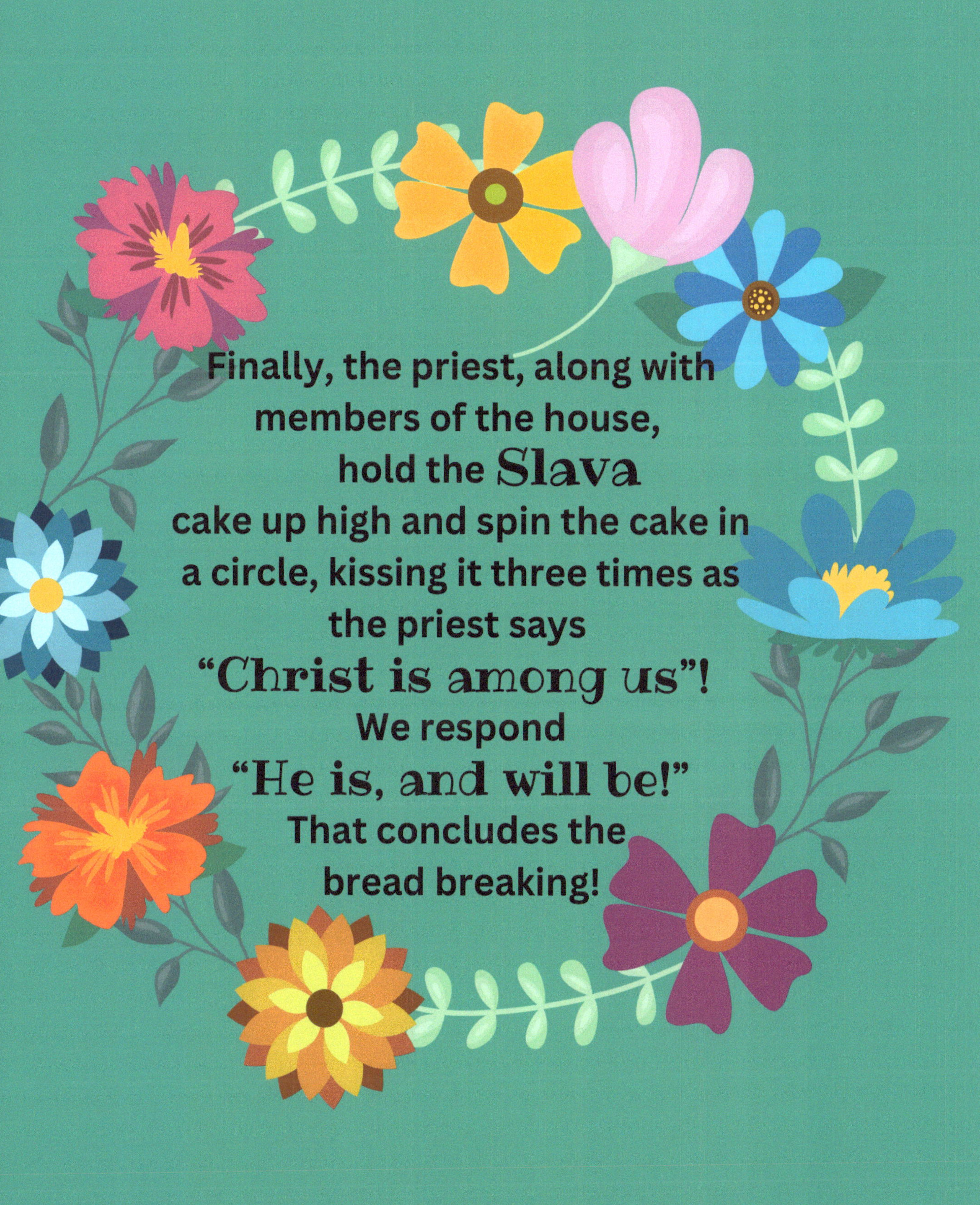

Finally, the priest, along with
members of the house,
hold the Slava
cake up high and spin the cake in
a circle, kissing it three times as
the priest says
"Christ is among us"!
We respond
"He is, and will be!"
That concludes the
bread breaking!

First, the sacred Slava candle is lit to remind us that Christ is the light of the world. Next, we sing a hymn to the family's patron saint and cut the Slava cake into the shape of a cross as it is poured with wine.

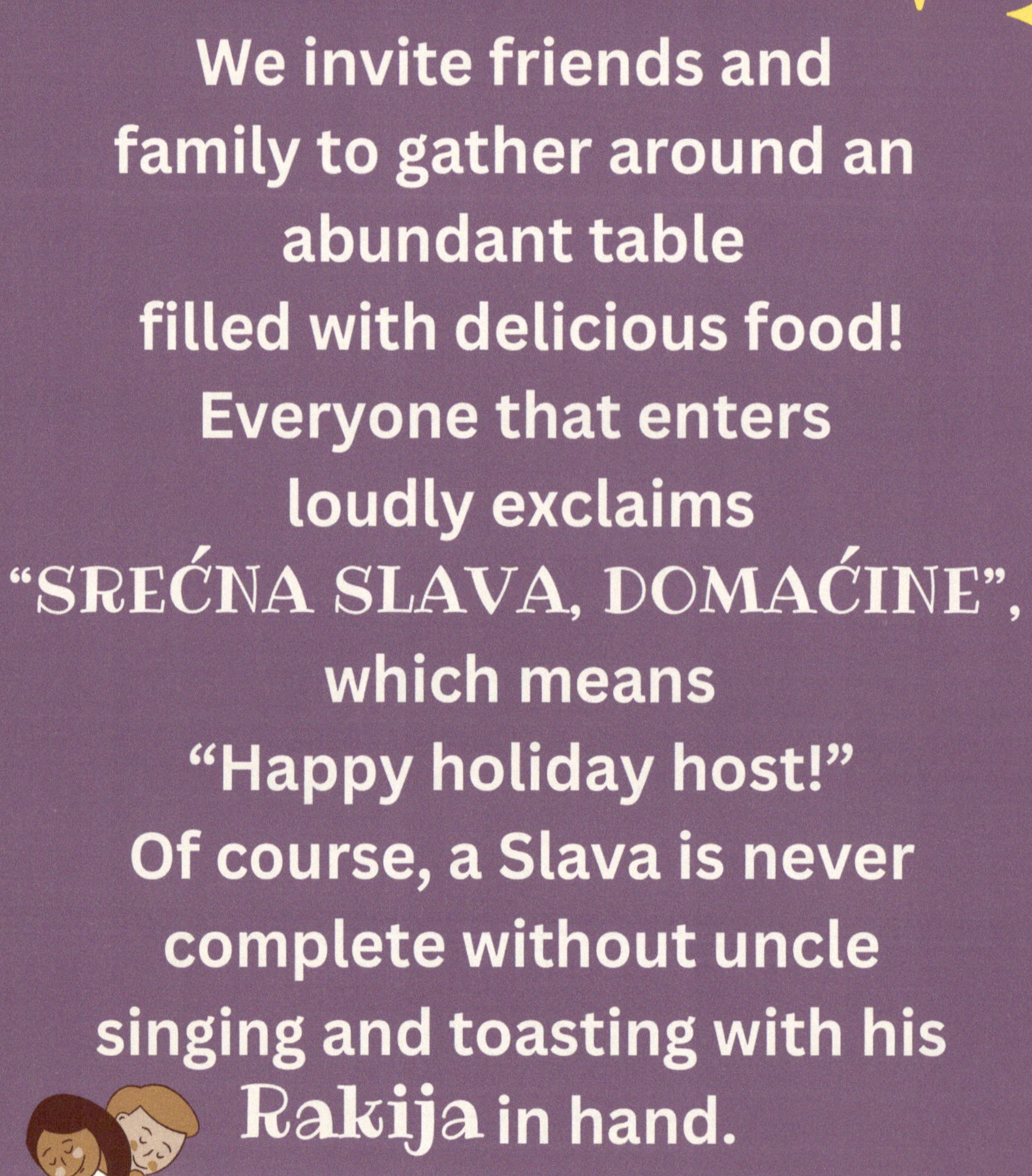

We invite friends and
family to gather around an
abundant table
filled with delicious food!
Everyone that enters
loudly exclaims
"SREĆNA SLAVA, DOMAĆINE",
which means
"Happy holiday host!"
Of course, a Slava is never
complete without uncle
singing and toasting with his
Rakija in hand.

At dinner, we exchange hugs
and kisses. Love and laughter
fills the air as we sing songs of
good health and security from
our protector.

We have honored our patron saint this year. We wish our loved ones many more Slavas to celebrate as we bid them a good night. We will celebrate and feast again next year!

"Where there is a Slava, there is a Serb!"

Father Predrag Bojovic

Father Predrag Bojovic was key in writing this children's book about Slava. Without his guidance this would not be possible.

He currently remains leading his church Saint Sava in San Gabriel.

After getting married in 2003 he was ordained into priesthood by Bishop Chrysostom of Zica and assigned to the Parish of Gornji Milanovac, Serbia, at The Holy Trinity Church but, also, put in charge of the Old Town church of Saint Nicholas the Wonderworker, which suffered greatly under the Communist Regime and needed extensive remodeling. After being neglected for almost 100 years and having irregular services, under the pastoral care of Fr. Predrag, this church was brought back to its old glory and became a very strong and vibrant liturgical Community.

My children baptized at Saint Sava of San Gabriel.

Thank you for reading! If you'd like to follow me scan the qr code below!

SERBIA

www.ingramcontent.com/pod-product-compliance
Lightning Source LLC
Chambersburg PA
CBHW041637110726
48005CB00002B/628